mN

Great Artists

Leonardo da Vinci

ABDO
Publishing Company

Joanne Mattern

visit us at
www.abdopub.com

Published by ABDO Publishing Company, 4940 Viking Drive, Edina, Minnesota 55435.
Copyright © 2005 by Abdo Consulting Group, Inc. International copyrights reserved in all
countries. No part of this book may be reproduced in any form without written permission
from the publisher. The Checkerboard Library™ is a trademark and logo of ABDO Publishing
Company.

Printed in the United States.

Cover Photo: Corbis
Interior Photos: Art Resource pp. 12, 14, 15, 17, 19; Corbis pp. 1, 4, 5, 9, 10, 11, 13, 18, 21,
    22, 23, 25, 26, 27, 28, 29

Series Coordinator: Megan Murphy
Editors: Stephanie Hedlund, Jennifer R. Krueger
Cover Design: Neil Klinepier
Interior Design: Dave Bullen

Library of Congress Cataloging-in-Publication Data

Mattern, Joanne, 1963 -
    Leonardo da Vinci / Joanne Mattern.
        p. cm. -- (Great artists)
    Includes index.
    ISBN 1-59197-842-4
    1. Leonardo, da Vinci, 1452-1519--Juvenile literature. 2. Artists--Italy--Biography--Juvenile
    literature. I. Title.

N6923.L33M377 2005
709'.2--dc22
[B]

                                                                    2004052804

Contents

Leonardo

Leonardo da Vinci is one of the most famous artists in history. He lived during a time called the **Renaissance**. During this period, people were very interested in art. Many famous paintings and sculptures were created during the Renaissance.

Leonardo did more than just paint. He was interested in how things worked. So, he was also a scientist and an **architect**. Leonardo studied the human body. He also designed palaces, machines, and flying devices.

But, Leonardo will always be remembered for his paintings. Some were portraits of living people. Others showed scenes from the Bible. People still admire Leonardo's artwork today. He is considered one of the most important artists who ever lived.

Leonardo's self-portrait

A drawing of Leonardo made in the 1800s. In addition to being a genius, he was also known as a handsome, friendly person.

Timeline

1452 ~ Leonardo was born in Vinci, Italy.

1474 ~ Leonardo painted *Madonna of the Carnation*.

1482 ~ Duke Sforza of Milan hired Leonardo to be the artist of his court.

1485 ~ Leonardo finished *The Virgin of the Rocks*.

1495 ~ Leonardo began the *Last Supper*.

1500 ~ Leonardo was welcomed back to Florence.

1501 ~ Leonardo began work on *Virgin and Child with St. Anne*.

1503 ~ Leonardo was commissioned for the *Battle of Anghiari* but did
not finish the work; Leonardo painted the *Mona Lisa*.

1506 ~ Leonardo began his second stay in Milan.

1513 ~ Leonardo went to Rome.

1516 ~ Leonardo moved to France.

1519 ~ Leonardo died in France on May 2.

Fun Facts

- One of Leonardo's notebooks, called the Leicester Codex, belongs to Bill Gates, the chairman of Microsoft. He paid more than $30 million for it!

- Leonardo spent a lot of time studying the way birds and bats fly. And, he dreamed of inventing a way for people to fly. His notebooks are filled with drawings of flying machines. No one knows if he ever tried any of them out.

- As an architect, Leonardo mainly gave advice to others. But, one of his drawings was actually created 500 years later! A bridge modeled after Leonardo's design was built in Norway in 2001.

- Some believe that Leonardo did not get along very well with Michelangelo. He was another famous artist working in Leonardo's time. They worked together on a project for a public building in Florence. But, the work was never completed.

A Boy from Vinci

Leonardo da Vinci was born on April 15, 1452, in a town called Vinci, Italy. It is near Florence. Today, the town is used as part of his name. *Da Vinci* means "from Vinci."

Not much is known about Leonardo's family. His father was a **notary** named Ser Piero. Ser Piero was an important man in Vinci. Leonardo's mother was a peasant named Caterina.

Leonardo's parents never married each other. So, Leonardo spent most of his childhood with his father's family. For many years, the boy lived with his grandfather.

As a child, Leonardo learned to read, write, and do math. But, he never learned to speak Latin very well. This was a very important language for educated people in Italy at the time. Still, his family saw great promise in young Leonardo.

No one knows exactly where Leonardo was born in Vinci.
But, there are many places that the locals claim to be his real birthplace!

In the Workshop

Leonardo was always good at drawing. So, Ser Piero thought that his son could be an artist. When Leonardo was about 15 years old, his father sent him to Florence. There, Leonardo worked as an **apprentice** for a famous artist named Andrea del Verrocchio.

Verrocchio encouraged his students to learn about all kinds of art, not just painting. The students even studied the art of machines. Leonardo lived in Verrocchio's workshop. He learned how to paint and sculpt there.

Verrocchio liked Leonardo and thought the young man was a good painter. So, he let Leonardo paint an angel in his *Baptism of Christ*. Many people thought this angel was the best part of the work!

Florence, Italy

Leonardo's angel is on the far left of Verrocchio's Baptism of Christ.

On His Own

Leonardo still lived with Verrocchio when he completed *Madonna of the Carnation* in 1474. This painting showed the Virgin Mary and the baby Jesus in front of a mountain scene. The public loved the painting. And, it was often imitated by other artists.

In 1477, Leonardo left Verrocchio to live on his own. He worked on several paintings over the next few years. Then in 1481, Leonardo was **commissioned** for a painting called *The Adoration of the Magi*.

Leonardo often began new projects and did not finish the ones he was working on. In 1482, Duke Ludovico Sforza of Milan presented him with a new opportunity. He hired Leonardo to be his artist. Leonardo stopped working on *The Adoration of the Magi* and moved to Milan.

Leonardo's **Madonna of the Carnation**

There, he began several projects for the duke and completed six paintings. One of these was called *The Virgin of the Rocks*. This work shows figures from the Bible, including the Virgin Mary, the baby Jesus, and John the Baptist. The work was finished in about 1485.

As in his other religious paintings, The Virgin of the Rocks *has hazy and soft colors. Leonardo often used this technique, called sfumato. In sfumato works, forms such as people are not outlined clearly. Instead, they blend into their surroundings.*

Renaissance Man

While Leonardo was in Milan, he didn't just work as an artist. He also advised others on subjects such as engineering and **architecture**. He filled thousands of notebook pages with thoughts and observations on everything from astronomy to the human body.

In his notebooks, Leonardo came up with inventions that could not be made at that time. For example, he designed an underwater breathing device, a helicopter, a submarine, and a tank. In this way, Leonardo was way ahead of his time!

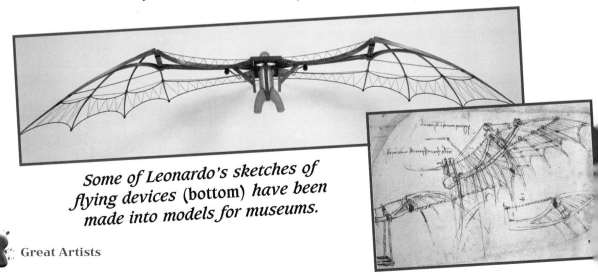

Some of Leonardo's sketches of flying devices (bottom) *have been made into models for museums.*

Leonardo wrote everything in his notebooks backward. He was probably not trying to keep his work secret. He eventually wanted people to read his notebooks. Some people think it was easier for Leonardo to write this way because he was left-handed.

Da Vinci Code

Leonardo liked to write backward. This type of writing is called mirror writing because it can easily be read with a mirror. For example, read the reflection of this text in a mirror and see what you find!

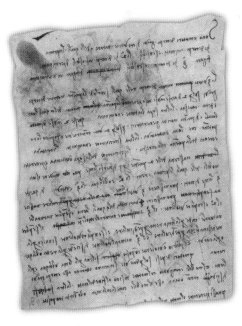

Give it a try. If you're left-handed, you may have a special talent for it, just like Leonardo. See! It's not so hard to read after all!

Last Supper

In 1495, Leonardo started to work on one of his most famous paintings. It was a **fresco** called the *Last Supper*. Leonardo painted it on the wall of the dining room in a monastery in Milan.

The *Last Supper* shows a famous scene from the Bible in which Jesus tells the **apostles** that one of them will betray him. The reactions of the apostles are captured by Leonardo's brush. His skill also shows how light and shadow fall on the figures around the table.

Leonardo liked to experiment with ways to apply paint to create different looks. For the *Last Supper*, he used egg **tempura** and painted it on dry plaster. But after the *Last Supper* was finished, the paint began flaking off the wall. Today, parts of the painting are hard to see.

The paint on Leonardo's Last Supper (bottom) was flaking, and the colors were fading. The original painting looked more like the restored version (top). The restoration project took 20 years and was completed in 1999.

Horse and Rider

In Milan, Leonardo also worked on a huge sculpture of Duke Sforza's father riding a horse. From 1482 to 1499, Leonardo developed this sculpture. For much of this time, he sketched horses. Then a large, clay model was made based on Leonardo's design.

That's as close as the work came to completion. Leonardo needed to **cast** the statue in bronze. But, the French army threatened to attack Milan. Instead of making a sculpture, the bronze was used to make weapons such as cannons.

In 1499, the French army invaded Milan. Leonardo's great clay horse was destroyed by the French army. His patron, Sforza, was captured. Later that year, Leonardo left the troubled city.

*One of Leonardo's
many horse sketches*

Leonardo didn't just honor Sforza's father with his work. He also painted Sforza's love! She is the woman in Lady with an Ermine.

Going Home

After leaving Milan, Leonardo visited the Italian city of Mantua. Then, he went to Venice. He helped the leaders of Venice plan military defenses.

Finally, Leonardo went back home to Florence in 1500. The people of Florence were happy to see him. He was very famous by then. And, the city was proud of him.

In 1501, Leonardo began working on a painting called the *Virgin and Child with St. Anne*. The painting depicts the Virgin Mary, the baby Jesus, and Saint Anne. In the Bible, Saint Anne is the mother of the Virgin Mary. Florentines loved the work.

In 1503, Leonardo was **commissioned** to paint a huge battle scene. It was called the *Battle of Anghiari*, and it would be on a building in Florence. He never finished the work. But that same year, Leonardo received another very important commission.

In 1502, Leonardo began working for an Italian general named Cesare Borgia. Leonardo made maps and helped Borgia with his military plans.

Mona Lisa

Francesco del Giocondo was an influential man in Florence. In 1503, Giocondo asked Leonardo to paint a picture of his wife. She was called Mona Lisa. Leonardo agreed, and the painting became one of the most famous in the world.

Because Mona Lisa was the wife of Giocondo, the *Mona Lisa* is sometimes called *La Gioconda*. It shows a young woman sitting on a balcony. The woman looks very calm and serious. But, her mouth looks like it is about to curve into a smile.

The **Mona Lisa**

There are many reproductions of the Mona Lisa, *such as this one on the side of a barn in Wisconsin!*

Leonardo's great skill made the woman in the painting look real. He used a style of painting called chiaroscuro. This term is a combination of the Italian words for light and dark. In this kind of painting, light and shadow are just as important as color.

Return to Milan

While in Florence, Leonardo spent a lot of time studying anatomy, or the body. Leonardo drew many sketches of bones, muscles, and organs. His pictures are more detailed than any other anatomy drawings of his time.

In 1506, Leonardo returned to Milan. At that time, Milan was under French control. The French governor of the city, Charles d'Amboise, had invited Leonardo back. D'Amboise paid Leonardo very well, and he respected the artist.

Leonardo did not paint many pictures during this time of his life. He was more interested in **architecture**, anatomy, and other areas of science. Leonardo was very happy in Milan. The governor allowed him to pursue his different interests.

Artist's Corner

Because Leonardo was so knowledgeable in many areas, people found it hard to describe his genius. So, the term *Renaissance Man* was created. It is used today to refer to someone with a wide range of abilities.

Leonardo was never interested in literature or religion. He was always fascinated in what he could see. This meant he was interested in architecture, anatomy, and even botany.

Leonardo probably planned to combine all of his writings and ideas into one theory on how to view the world. He never accomplished this. But, he serves as a model today for everyone who is curious and observant.

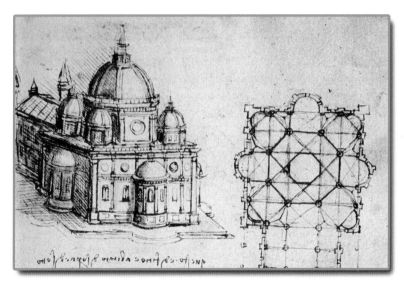

This cathedral is one of Leonardo's many architectural drawings.

Final Years

In 1513, the French were forced to leave Milan. At 60 years old, Leonardo also fled the political troubles in the city. He spent three years in Rome. There he worked for Giuliano de Medici, the brother of Pope Leo X.

Many artists were working in Rome at the time. Leonardo did not have many **commissions**. In addition, his father died. Leonardo was always fighting with his half brothers and half sisters over their father's money and possessions.

Leonardo was lonely. He had never married or had children of his own. Instead, he cared for his **apprentices**, including Francesco Melzi. Melzi was very good to Leonardo in return. He stayed with him until Leonardo died.

In 1516, King Francis I invited Leonardo to come to France. Leonardo

Giuliano de Medici

was happy to accept. King Francis and Leonardo became good friends. Leonardo enjoyed working for him. He planned a palace and garden for the king. He also continued to study, write, and invent.

King Francis I was a generous patron and allowed Leonardo to study freely in the last years of his life.

Leonardo Today

Leonardo died in France on May 2, 1519. He left most of his possessions to his **apprentice**, Melzi. Leonardo was buried at the palace church. Later, the church and many of its graves were destroyed. Today, the exact location of Leonardo's grave is not known.

Many of Leonardo's paintings did not survive either. There are only 17 of his paintings left. And, not all of them are finished. Other paintings were badly damaged or lost over the years. Many of Leonardo's notebooks were lost, too.

An etching of Leonardo

The chateau of Francis I was Leonardo's last home.

In spite of these losses, the world still remembers Leonardo da Vinci. The *Last Supper* and the *Mona Lisa* are two of the most loved paintings in the world. Scientists are amazed at Leonardo's scientific work as well. He was a man of true genius who gave the world many incredible gifts.

Glossary

apostle - any early Christian leader, especially the original 12 selected by Jesus to preach his word.

apprentice - a person who learns a trade or craft from a skilled worker.

architect - a person who plans and designs buildings. His or her work is called architecture.

cast - to form a shape by molding and then separating material from an object.

commission - a request to complete a work, such as a painting, for a certain person. To be commissioned is to be given such a request.

fresco - the art of painting on a wet surface that becomes hard when dry, such as a plaster wall.

notary - a person who specializes in making sure legal documents are real and not forged.

Renaissance - a revival of art and learning that began in Italy during the fourteenth century, marked by a renewed interest in Greek and Latin literature and art.

tempura - paint that uses something other than oil, such as egg yolk, to mix with dye.

Saying It

Andrea del Verrocchio - ahn-DREH-ah DALE vayr-RAWK-kyoh

chiaroscuro - kee-ahr-uh-SKYUR-oh

D'Amboise - dahn-BWAHZ

Francesco del Giocondo - frahn-CHAYS-koh DALE joh-KOHN-doh

Giuliano de Medici - jool-YAHN-oh DAY MEHD-ee-chee

Ludovico Sforza - loo-doh-VEE-koh SFOHRT-sah

Vinci - VEEN-chee

Web Sites

To learn more about Leonardo da Vinci, visit ABDO Publishing Company on the World Wide Web at **www.abdopub.com**. Web sites about Leonardo are featured on our Book Links page. These links are routinely monitored and updated to provide the most current information available.

Index